M000238956

IMAGES
of America

ICEBREAKING
ALASKA

ON THE COVER: The Coast Guard cutter (CGC) *Northwind* (WAGB-282) breaks ice on its Arctic West deployment in 1967 as the crew watches. (Author's collection.)

IMAGES
of America

ICEBREAKING
ALASKA

Capt. Jeffrey D. Hartman, USCG (Retired)

ARCADIA
PUBLISHING

Copyright © 2014 by Capt. Jeffrey D. Hartman, USCG (Retired)
ISBN 978-1-4671-3108-7

Published by Arcadia Publishing
Charleston, South Carolina

Printed in the United States of America

Library of Congress Control Number: 2013953694

For all general information, please contact Arcadia Publishing:
Telephone 843-853-2070
Fax 843-853-0044
E-mail sales@arcadiapublishing.com
For customer service and orders:
Toll-Free 1-888-313-2665

Visit us on the Internet at www.arcadiapublishing.com

This book is dedicated to the US Coast Guard icebreaking men and women and to their spouses who support them, especially to my late wife and partner, Lt. (j.g.) Sylvia Rojas Hartman, US Navy Reserve.

CONTENTS

ACKNOWLEDGMENTS

The author's great appreciation for the assistance with information and/or pictures in this book goes to Jennifer A. Gaudio, US Coast Guard (USCG) Academy Museum curator; Capt. Gene Davis, director of Coast Guard Museum Northwest; Ens. Rebecca Follmer, CGC *Healy* public information officer; Dr. Robert Browning, Coast Guard Headquarters historian; Rear Adm. Doug Teeson, USCG (retired); Ned Lofton; Virgil Keith; and especially, Aviation Electrician Senior Chief (AECS) John Furqueron.

INTRODUCTION

The Alaskan Arctic is a place that most people will never see. It is a barren, seemingly lifeless place, with great challenges even to survive. Yet the Arctic has a rich, complex history and has great promise for the future. It has been the home of the Native peoples for thousands of years. These ancient peoples, known as Ipani, or "long-time-ago Eskimos," lived by adapting to a substance lifestyle harvesting whales, seals, and birds when they were available. This subsistence lifestyle was carefully taught to each new generation. This balanced, traditional way of life has been overtaken by modern civilization with its much greater hunger for resources. Many now claim the resources of the Arctic.

There are five major players in the Arctic that border the semi-enclosed Arctic Ocean. The United States has eight percent of this pie. The largest segment belongs to Russia with 44 percent. Canada is next with 23 percent. Denmark, because of Greenland, is third largest with 13 percent. Norway follows the United States at seven percent, and five percent is open water.

The allure of the Arctic to the nonnative has changed over time. Early on, the quest was discovery. Where could one go? When could one go there? Was there an open ocean somewhere in the middle? Gradually these questions were answered. But the history of the Arctic is fairly recent. It was only a little over a century ago that a Westerner sailed through the Northwest Passage. There have been historic disasters and great mysteries and survival under extreme conditions throughout the region's history.

The Arctic has changed dramatically. It has been discovered but sparsely chartered. We know that it has vast riches in oil and natural gas. Slightly over 100 years ago, it was a rich whaling ground to which American ships flocked. Many never came back.

The Arctic itself is changing. The thick ice is getting thinner. The new ice each year is retreating further from shore. Many nations now see the Arctic as a shortcut to markets. In some ways, the Arctic is less predictable and hence more dangerous than in the past. Barrow has 324 days of freezing temperatures every year. It is still a place of intense storms, and oddly enough, less ice close to shore means that windblown waves have the potential of greater destructive power. Also, no matter how much the ice retreats in the warmer periods, it always comes back in the Arctic winter. So any structure that is not temporary needs to be built to withstand the winter and the force of moving ice.

For years, US Navy and US Coast Guard icebreakers have come to the Arctic to learn, research, and discover and to support national objectives. The Coast Guard has broad responsibilities as the federal onsite presence to protect the mariner and the environment but also to facilitate the nation's commerce. Much of this requires icebreakers. This book is about the how and why of icebreaking in Alaska. Opinions expressed are my own and not official Coast Guard policy.

Despite the dramatic changes occurring or forecast for the Arctic, the nation has but one Polar-class icebreaker operational, the USCGC *Polar Star* (WAGB-10), and one medium icebreaker, the *Healy* (WAGB-20). Both are home-ported in Seattle, as is the sister ship to the *Polar Star*, the *Polar Sea* (WAGB-11), which is in mothballs for lack of funding.

For a time, icebreakers were a high national priority. World War II logistics required the ability to keep ports and waterways open in the winter months. This included sub-polar regions in Greenland and Labrador. For this duty, the *Storis* was commissioned in 1942. Funding for the Wind-class breakers was authorized; however, the first three of the new icebreakers were promptly loaned to our ally Russia, which had a crucial need for the war effort against the Nazis. These were the icebreakers *Northwind*, *Southwind*, and *Westwind*. The fourth cutter in the series, *Eastwind*, stayed with the United States and was operated by the Coast Guard during the war.

Additional breakers were built, including the *Edisto* and *Burton Island*, which were operated by the Navy. Also a second *Northwind* was constructed to replace the loaner to the Russians and was operated by the Coast Guard. In 1951–1952, the three loaned icebreakers were returned by the Russians, and two became Navy icebreakers *Atka* and *Staten Island*. The third loaner was the *Westwind*, which was to be operated by the Coast Guard.

In April 1967, the US Department of Transportation was created by the Johnson administration. The Coast Guard left its home in the US Treasury Department where it had been for 177 years to join the new department. As part of the transfer, the Coast Guard was given the responsibility to operate all the nation's icebreakers. At the time, this inventory included the icebreakers *Northwind*, *Westwind*, *Eastwind*, *Southwind*, *Edisto*, *Atka*, *Staten Island*, *Burton Island*, and *Glacier*.

Herein, we will see the beauty and bravery of these great ships and their crews. We will see the conditions under which they did their work. Also we will see what their work was and why it was necessary. Tragedies will be documented so that we can learn from them. By studying the past, we hope to be able to forecast what is to come. Let's get started. Let's break the ice.

One

DEFINING ALASKA
ICEBREAKING

The saltwater area known as the Arctic is considered the seas north of the Aleutian Islands, including the Bering Sea, the Arctic Ocean, the Chukchi Sea, and the Beaufort Sea. Not many of these waters contain ice all the time, but they all have contained ice in the past some of the time. Typically, winter sea ice extends to Nunivac Island.

An important fact to remember is that sea ice is not stationary. It is blown by the wind and moved by currents. Different forces can move ice in different directions. Where two sheets of ice meet under pressure, giant ridges of ice can form. The moving ice can separate and create open water between the flows of ice. These are known as leads. Ships can make good progress following leads, but they can close just as fast as they open.

Special-purpose ships that are designed to operate in the ice are called icebreakers. These ships have three characteristics not found on other ships. They have specially strengthened hulls to withstand the pressure of the ice, a unique hull with a bow designed to ride up on the ice, and an ice-clearing shape. Finally, they have extra power for pushing the ship through the ice.

Alaska, the other half of the title, is also unique. It is one-fifth the size of the United States, yet the fewest residents of all the states except for Wyoming. Of these occupants, nearly half are in Anchorage. The state contains six regions, Alaska Peninsula, Aleutians, Bering Sea Coast, Interior, South-Central/Gulf Coast, and Southeast.

Logistics are a major concern here. From the Coast Guard Air Station on Kodiak Island, it is over 1,000 miles to Barrow and over 1,200 to Attu Island. There are three major mountain ranges. There are no roads to Barrow, Nome, Kotzebue, Bethel, Dillingham, and many others, including, surprisingly, the capital of Juneau. Most Alaskan communities depend on ocean-borne commerce. Flying fuel into Nome rather than coming by sea would be cost prohibitive even for rich Alaska. An important fact is that Alaska is a maritime state.

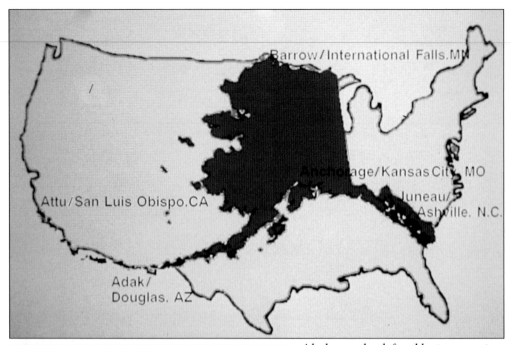

Barrow/International Falls.MN

Anchorage/Kansas City. MO

Juneau/
Ashville. N.C.

Attu/San Luis Obispo.CA

Adak/
Douglas. AZ

Alaska can be defined by its great size. This map of Alaska superimposed on the Lower 48 provides a vivid image of the challenges of providing logistics in the Great Land. Several Alaskan communities are paired with the geographical counterparts in the Lower 48. Keep in mind that none of the Alaskan communities are connected to each other by road. (Courtesy of USCG District No. 17 public information officer.)

This picture is of the Barrow airstrip in 1967 with the Distant Early Warning (DEW) Line station in the background. Barrow is now home to over 4,000 Alaskans. All of their groceries, fuel, medication, and so on have to come in either by air or sea. The delivery by sea is complicated because the sea is very shallow within a couple of miles of the beach. (Author's collection.)

Delivery by sea is difficult because none of the northern cities have suitable ports. The *Northwind* had a draft of about 29 feet, which necessitated anchoring some two miles off the beach in order for shore parties to visit Nome, shown here. The situation was the same in Barrow. (Author's collection.)

The historic revenue cutter *Bear* is pictured here in the ice off of Point Barrow. (Courtesy of Alaska State Library, US Revenue Cutter Service Collection.)

Alaska is known for its wonderful abundance of delicacies from the sea. (Author's collection.)

It is also defined by its potential for disasters, which this former fish processor exemplifies in Kodiak. The 1964 tsunami pushed the ship so far inland that it could not be refloated, and it was made into a nightclub and named the Beachcomber. (Author's collection.)

Alaska has extremes in weather. This approach to the Kodiak Airport in heavy winds requires a sturdy aircraft, a brave pilot, and luck. (Author's collection.)

Certainly, Alaska's wonderful beauty is well known. Here, a Coast Guard C-130 Hercules aircraft takes off on a mission from Kodiak Air Station with Pyramid Mountain in the background. (Courtesy of USCG District No. 17 public information officer.)

The challenge for Arctic mariners is obvious from this picture of weathered ice, which has been forced into pressure ridges by the wind and currents. If a ship becomes trapped in ice, such as this, where movement either forward or astern is blocked, dynamite is used to break the ship loose. (Courtesy of University of Alaska, Fairbanks, R.J. Leusen Photograph Collection UAF-2004-93-16.)

The special-purpose ships designed to operate in ice are the icebreakers. The Coast Guard designation for these workhorses is WAGB. Pictured is one of the famous Wind class, the CGC *Southwind* WAGB-280. Limited icebreakers make it difficult to support ice operations in both polar regions. Five of the vessels were built during World War II. They were 269 feet long, with a beam of 63 feet and a draft of 29 feet. With her tanks topped off, the *Northwind* could sail over 32,000 miles. (Courtesy of Dr. Robert Browning, Coast Guard Headquarters historian.)

This model of the wartime *Northwind* is in the Coast Guard Northwest Maritime Museum. The unique slopping bow is obvious. An unusual feature is the bow propeller. Not used normally for propulsion, they were intended to draw water from under the ice, allowing the breaker to more easily break the ice. (Author's collection.)

This beautiful model is of the historic revenue cutter *Bear*. She was a wooden vessel, but one designed to operate in icy waters. At 198 feet long and 30 feet wide, she had a combined propulsion package steam boiler and sail. Launched in 1874 as a sealer in Dundee, Scotland, she was commissioned in the Revenue Cutter Service in 1885 and served with distinction until 1929, a total of 44 years. She continued to be of value until lost in a storm off of New England under tow to be a floating restaurant. (Author's collection.)

The *Bear* is pictured where she was most at home, in the Arctic. In all, she spent 41 years flying the Revenue Cutter flag, protecting the mariners, the Native people, and the Alaskan Arctic. (Courtesy of Dr. Robert Browning, Coast Guard Headquarters historian.)

A polar bear hung in the Naval Arctic Research Lab (NARL) at Point Barrow; it was shot in the town dump and was cited as a nuisance bear. Polar bears are likely to become even more aggressive as the ice retreats and their seal-hunting opportunities decrease. (Author's collection.)

The Natives traditionally are whale hunters, and it is an important subsistence food for them as well as a cultural tradition. The structure in the background is built from whalebones. (Courtesy of the University of Washington Library.)

17

Helicopters, such as the HH-13N shown here, are important tools for the icebreakers. They are used as the eyes of the conning officer to check out leads in the ice to make sure they do not become blind alleys with giant pressure ridges. They can also provide important logistics such as picking up the mail. (Author's collection.)

Bags of mail are picked up to fly back to the *Northwind.* In these days before satellites, mail was the only way to keep up with the family back home. (Author's collection.)

The HH-52A, shown here on approach, replaced the "Bubble Bell." The HH-52 had greatly expanded capabilities and carrying capacity. The icebreaker aviation detachments operated two of these helicopters. (Courtesy of USCG District No. 17 public information officer.)

As the HH-52 was retired, the standard for shipboard deployment helicopters became the HH-65A and later models. (Courtesy of USCG District No. 17 public information officer.)

The headquarters for the Coast Guard in Alaska is in Juneau, the state capital. This picture was taken across Gastineau Channel from Douglas Island. The headquarters of the 17th Coast Guard District is in the federal office building, the nine-story building on the left side of the picture. (Author's collection.)

The eighth floor of the state office building in Juneau contains this wonderful story totem pole, a mounted brown bear, and a huge pipe organ on which free concerts are given on Friday at lunch hour. (Author's collection.)

Copyright, 1911. By Thwaites, J.E. 5-90

Revenue Cutter, Rush, In Bering Sea. Photo. From Deck Of Mail Steamer, Dora.

This picture of the revenue cutter (R/C) *Rush* is representative of the icebreaking program in heavy seas. (Courtesy of Alaska State Library, Arthur L. Agren Collection.)

The *Northwind* patch, proudly worn by crew on their flight jackets, is a picture of the past. (Courtesy of AECS John Furqueron.)

The *Bear* and the *Corwin* are seen here anchored in the ice off of Nome. (Courtesy of University of Alaska, Fairbanks, R.J. Leusen Collection.)

The *Northwind* rammed up on the ice to enable the engineers to weld a crack in the bow. The Arctic is a place of great challenge for the 15,000 Alaskans who live above the Arctic Circle and for those who come there for its riches. (Courtesy of Mike Studley.)

The welfare of the Eskimos must always be an important consideration in any activity in the Arctic. Their way of life is closely tied to land and the Arctic animals. They are American citizens and rightful shareholders in the Far North. (Courtesy of the USCG Academy Library.)

This practice was known as a whale dance. Perhaps it originated in tossing someone into the air to look for whale spouts. It is commonly done now as a tourist amusement called a Native blanket toss. (Courtesy of the USCG Academy Library.)

23

This 1911 picture of a group of Eskimo children on Little Diomede Island reflects their delicate beauty but also the fragile shyness of the people. This image was taken from scrapbook about Coast Guard cutter *Bertholf*. (Courtesy of the USCG Academy Library.)

The Revenue Cutter ships distributed government supplies to the Eskimos. Note the bird in the waistband of the boy pointing with his finger. (Courtesy of the USCG Academy Library.)

Two

DIAMONDS IN THE ARCTIC

Even with its desolation and harsh environs, the Arctic has things of great value. These "diamonds" have changed over time. A century and a half ago, it was whale oil that brought wooden ships and iron men all the way from New Bedford, Massachusetts, and other US seaports. These men came to know the Arctic, but they often did not treat it or its aboriginal people with respect. The survival of the whales was considered immaterial in regards to the profits to be made.

Whaling voyages were complex. They normally lasted for two years, sailing from the Northeast ports around the Cape of Good Hope. Despite this, in 1852, there were 200 whaling ships hunting the great mammals. As whale numbers diminished and became harder to find, the prey became the walrus, which was also a source of oil and much easier to hunt. A single rifleman could kill an entire herd basking on the ice. It is estimated that 100,000 walrus were taken by 1880.

The next thing to attract the exploiters to the Arctic was gold. Nome, although south of the Arctic Circle, has to contend with ice three quarters of the year. Despite this, Nome was the location of the largest Alaskan gold rush from 1898 to 1904. At its peak, there were over 20,000 people in Nome, making it Alaska's largest city at the time by far.

Petroleum exploration was the next big thing. There are 19 geological basins in the Arctic region. Only half of these basins have been explored. The US Geological Survey estimated in 2008 that there are 90 billion barrels of oil and 44 billion of natural gas liquids north of the Arctic Circle. Getting it out and to market safely is the great challenge.

For the Inupiat, their Arctic diamonds are the food, clothing, and shelter materials from the land and sea that they have gathered for thousands of years. Money means little if there is little of value to spend it on. They have adopted some technologies, such as snow machines and outboard motors, but the goals remain the same. That is their traditional subsistence lifestyle. Their greatest fear is that the search by others for their diamonds will destroy their own.

The last diamond is not really a tangible thing but rather a process. It is the long-sought-after passage from one market to another. Being able to cut through the Arctic is much shorter, thus cheaper and quicker. It may not be far off that this is possible at least part of the year. As 90 percent of what people consume comes by marine transportation, the reduction in time and cost to bring these products to market is of great value.

The executive officer of the *Northwind*, Cmdr. Stu Beckwith, stands with some Eskimo children in the lobby of a Nome hotel. The ancient ancestors of these children came to the frozen area over 5,000 years ago. What brought them? No one knows for sure. Possibly they were following migrating animals of the time in search of food, furs, and the support they provide. Perhaps they were just curious like the many who came after them. (Author's collection.)

The Eskimos follow their traditional subsistence lifestyle but use some modern tools like rifles, motorcycles, and snowmobiles. Alaska again is unusual in that it has officially established the subsistence gathering of fish and game a priority for the rural Natives. The majority of this is fish (60 percent) followed by land mammals (20 percent) and marine mammals (14 percent). Birds, shellfish, and plants each account for two percent of the subsistence total. In 1967, the outskirts of these remote villages would be bordered with discarded machines that had broken down and were too expensive to fix. (Courtesy of the USCG Academy Museum, Rush/Shepard Collection.)

Surely diamonds of the Arctic must include the special people that have lived there and prospered for centuries. The famous Arctic captain Mike Healy thought so. Here, he is pictured second from right in the front row with a bridal couple in their finest onboard the *Bear*. (Courtesy of the USCG Academy Museum.)

The revenue cutter *Bear* was much appreciated by Eskimos and mariners in distress. She assisted them over her decades of Arctic duty. (Courtesy of the USCG Academy Museum, Dempwolf Collection.)

Native people created wonderful works of art, such as totems and ivory carvings, throughout Alaska. (Courtesy of the USCG Academy Museum.)

The wonderful baskets were so tight that they could carry water in some cases. (Courtesy of the USCG Academy Museum.)

Whales first attracted large numbers of outsiders in 1848. The success of the early attempts prompted a fast response, and the 1852 season saw over 200 whaling ships involved that resulted in a catch of $14 million. These were rough ventures, often lasting two years away from home. The products were whale oil, which was used in lamps, and baleen. The whale filters food from seawater using the baleen. Depending on the species of whale, the baleen can be up to 11 feet long. It is strong and flexible. Products it was used for included corset stays, collar stiffeners, parasol ribs, and buggy whips. Pictured here, crew members from the revenue cutter *Itasca* observe the whaling processing on Akutan. The blubber from the whale was cut into manageable-sized pieces and then rendered into oil by boiling. The smell was reputed to be overwhelming. After extensive hunting, the whales became scarce in the mid-1900s, and the hunt turned to walrus, which were also a good source of oil. They were also easier to kill. A rifleman could take an entire herd on an ice flow. In the third quarter of the 19th century, over 100,000 walrus were slaughtered. (Courtesy of the Coast Guard Museum Northwest.)

The sea lions were plentiful and easy to kill. (Courtesy of the USCG Academy Museum, Rush/ Shepard Collection.)

The taking of seal hides was brutal but effective. One of the first jobs for the revenue cutters like the *Rush* was to control the sealing harvest. (Courtesy of the USCG Academy Museum, Rush/ Shepard Collection.)

Unalaska, also known as Dutch Harbor, was an important location for the revenue cutters. This was where they could get coal and supplies. It was also the headquarters for the Bering Sea Patrol, shown here. The Coast Guard official song, "Semper Paratus," was written here. (Courtesy of the USCG Academy Museum, Claude Marrow Collection.)

The *Bear* takes a break at Dutch Harbor in the Aleutians. (Courtesy of the USCG Academy Museum, Waesche Collection.)

The next event that brought large numbers to the Arctic was the Nome gold rush from 1899 to 1909. At its peak, there were over 20,000 people in Nome, making it the largest city in Alaska by far. The output is estimated to have been 112 metric tons of the precious metal. (Courtesy of Alaska State Library, Robert Pittenger Collection.)

The shallowness of the water off Nome required that people and cargo be lightered ashore in small boats. The frequent high winds made this a dangerous operation. The picture shows the damage caused by a storm. A Coast Guard lifeboat station was established in Nome to provide a rescue capability to pluck the hapless from the freezing waters. (Courtesy of the Coast Guard Museum Northwest.)

This Eskimo family is being transported on a revenue cutter. (Courtesy of the USCG Academy Museum.)

This picture was taken in 1967 showing the development of Nome. The population is listed in the *Alaska Almanac 33rd Edition* as 3,620 in 2010. (Author's collection.)

This is the main street of Nome, pictured in 1967. (Author's collection.)

This lovely Eskimo woman posed for a professional studio portrait in Nome. (Courtesy of the USCG Academy Museum, Dempwolf Collection.)

This is a very early picture of Juneau. Joe Juneau and his partner Richard Harris, who were actually led to the site by a local Indian chief, established it as a result of the discovery of gold. (Courtesy of the USCG Academy Museum.)

The entrance to Port Townsend Bay was guarded by Fort Flagler on Marrowstone Island. Port Townsend was an important seaport supporting the Alaska Patrol revenue cutters. (Courtesy of the USCG Academy.)

A liberty boat was used for going to and from Nome. The *Northwind* was required to anchor several miles offshore because of the shallowness of the water. The water and the increasing intensity of the Arctic storms often batter the city. (Author's collection.)

Many attempts have been made to traverse the famed Northwest Passage. One of the most extensive was the $40-million attempt, funded by Humble Oil, by the supertanker SS *Manhattan* in 1969 escorted by the Canadian icebreaker CCGS *John A. MacDonald* and the USCG icebreaker *Northwind*. In the picture, the ice trapped the tanker for two days. The convoy eventually made it, but the idea of ice-reinforced tankers to take North Slope oil to market was abandoned. (Courtesy of Virgil Keith.)

One of the most elusive of the Alaska Arctic treasures is the ability to use its location to reduce distances between continents. Going over the top is a much shorter distance between points than longitudinally. As 90 percent of consumer products come by ship, this could mean a great savings in fuel and time to get things to market. If one imagines a clock face superimposed on the North Pole, Alaska is at 10:00 to 10:30. Russia would run from 11:00 around to 4:00, where Norway is. Greenland would be at the 6:30. Natives at times came aboard along this route, as pictured here on the *Bear* in St. Lawrence Bay off the coast of Siberia. (Courtesy of the USCG Academy Museum.)

The *Northwind* attempted to escort the *Manhattan* but had to drop out due to an engine problem. This picture shows a beating that the *Northwind* took in breaking the ice. (Courtesy of Rear Adm. Doug Teeson.)

Another location advantage of the Arctic is that it is "Top Cover for North America," as the Alaskan Command proudly says. This was evident in the Distant Early Warning (DEW) Line's 58 radar stations constructed across the top of Alaska and Canada. Ordered by President Eisenhower, these were constructed in 1955–1957. The resupply of the manned stations was accomplished with the assistance of US and Canadian icebreakers. (Author's collection.)

Perhaps the ultimate diamond of the Arctic is just the challenge it offers. It is like no place on Earth with great beauty and great danger. (Courtesy of Ens. Rebecca Follmer, CGC *Healy* public information officer.)

The Native people must always be considered. The woman pictured here was an Eskimo princess named Ootkumunga, daughter of Teneskan, according to the photographer. (Courtesy of the USCG Academy Museum.)

Too often, the well-meaning civilized society has broken up families by sending off the Native children to schools far from their parents and homes. (Courtesy of the USCG Academy Museum.)

Three

DANGERS OF THE ARCTIC

The Arctic offers jewels of great value for different people and different reasons. These jewels come with risks as well. It is a land of isolation and a long way from help for those who get into trouble. There is extreme weather, and even with global warming, ice covers much of it year-round.

From the mariner's point of view, there are only two types of ice. They are sea ice and glacial ice. Sea ice forms when the temperature gets cold enough to freeze the surface of the water. New ice that forms each year is white and relatively weak. As it ages, it loses its salt content, changes into different colors, and can become harder than stone. Glacial ice is generally ice formed by thousands of years of snow falling on continental land. It gradually is pressed into ice and can break off in pieces from the land and become icebergs. Alaska does not have icebergs, such as the one that sank the *Titanic*, but there are many dangers facing the unwary.

The history of the Arctic is replete with stories of disasters. The British government early on had offered a prize of 20,000 pounds sterling to the discoverer of the Northwest Passage, and many intrepid would-be explorers tried to collect it. Many died trying. In 1845, Sir John Franklin took an expedition of 134 men on two ships into the ice never to be seen alive again. Some of the bodies were recovered after a massive search. All had died of starvation and exposure.

The whaling period brought many men and ships and more disasters. The worst year was 1871, when 32 whaling ships were trapped when the ice pack shifted unexpectedly in a storm. Amazingly, 1,200 whalers were able to cross 60 miles of ice and open water pushing small boats before they were taken aboard ships that had not been trapped. The abandoned 32 whaling ships were never recovered.

In 1876, a total of 12 whaling ships had the same misfortune and became trapped. Some of the crew elected to stay with the ships hoping for the ice to release them, and 53 other sailors decided to walk out. Those men reached shore, where they wintered over with Eskimos. The trapped ships and their crew were never seen again, likely crushed by the ice.

The Revenue Cutter Service rescued many a distressed mariner and assisted the Native peoples. Shown are the cutters *Perry*, *Rush*, *Bear*, and *Thetis* moored at Unalaska. (Courtesy of the USCG Academy Museum.)

One of the most famous of the Arctic tragedies was that of the USS *Jeannette*, commanded by Lt. Cmdr. George DeLong. Trapped in pack ice for nearly two years, the crew of 33 abandoned the ship and attempted to walk out pulling small boats. A total of 21 souls, including DeLong, died from starvation or exposure. A monument to DeLong was established at the US Naval Academy in Annapolis. (Courtesy of the US Navy.)

Whalers had a very negative impact on the Eskimo lifestyle. The disrupting of the traditional subsistence food gathering led to starvation of some villages. Rev. Sheldon Jackson, a Presbyterian missionary and the federal commissioner for Native education, recognized the problem and helped to resolve it. (Courtesy of Alaska State Library, Shelton Jackson Collection.)

(Photo by La Roche, Seattle, May 15, 1899.)

REV. SHELDON JACKSON, D. D., LL. D.,
Vice President Alaska Geographical Society.

Capt. Mike Healy was a prominent Revenue Cutter skipper who partnered with Reverend Jackson. Together, they were largely responsible for the importation of reindeer from Siberia for the Alaskan Natives. (Courtesy of Dr. Robert Browning, Coast Guard Headquarters historian.)

Reverend Jackson was a very important figure in Alaskan history. He not only established and manned Native schools but through the reindeer program also established a year-round food supply and introduced a more stable way of life. He also had considerable influence on Alaska federal policy through a close relationship with President McKinley. (Courtesy of Alaska State Library, Alaska Native Organizations Collection.)

The logistics of transporting the reindeer were complicated. They had to be brought to the anchored *Bear*, hoisted aboard, kept calm on the cutter while transporting across the Bering Straits, then offloaded into small boats and transported ashore at the Native schools. (Courtesy of USCG District No. 17 public information officer.)

Jackson obtained congressional approval and church funding for purchase of Siberian reindeer to establish herds at the Native schools. Captain Healy provided transportation for the reindeer onboard the R/C *Bear*. Over a five-year period, over 1,200 head were transported successfully. (Courtesy of Dr. Robert Browning, Coast Guard Headquarters historian.)

The Siberian reindeer were smaller than caribou but in many cases were trained to carry loads and pull sleds. Here a R/C sailor tries one on for size. (Courtesy of USCG District No. 17 public information officer.)

The picture is of some of the trapped whalers at Point Barrow. The reindeer played an important part in a dramatic rescue known as the Overland Expedition. During the last week of September 1897, the ice moved in early, catching eight whaling ships by surprise. Once the owners of the ships and the newspapers in San Francisco heard of the plight of the whalers, they asked the president to do something. The answer was the Revenue Cutter icebreaker *Bear*. (Courtesy of USCG District No. 17 public information officer.)

The revenue cutter *Bear* had a reinforced hull, but her ability to break ice was limited due to lack of power. There was no way she could make it all the way through the ice to Point Barrow. (Courtesy of University of Alaska, Fairbanks, Emile Krulish Collection.)

This is the original chart of the *Bear* track involved with the Overland Expedition. It shows as far north that the *Bear* could go to attempt to rescue the trapped whalers because of the ice edge. Again it is important to keep in mind how far things are in Alaska. The distance from where the rescue party was put ashore to Point Barrow was over 1,500 miles. Another important point is that they went ashore in December, and much of the trip would be north of the Arctic Circle with no sun. (Courtesy of University of Alaska, Fairbanks, Rare Maps Collection.)

This was the volunteer *Bear* crew for the attempted rescue. Capt. Francis Tuttle, with the walrus mustache, had relieved Captain Healy. To the right of him is the leader of the expedition, 1st Lt. D.H. Jarvis. Jarvis was particularly well qualified to lead the party. He spoke Eskimo and was a seasoned Arctic expert. (Courtesy of USCG District No. 17 public information officer.)

The three main figures involved in the Overland Expedition are, from right to left, Jarvis, surgeon S.J. Call, and 2nd Lt. E.P. Bertholf. The latter was to become the commandant of the Coast Guard when it was formed from the Revenue Cutter Service and the Lifesaving Service in 1915. (Courtesy of USCG District No. 17 public information officer.)

This crew had the luxury of a full ensemble on board. (Courtesy of the USCG Academy Museum.)

Pictured here is a type of Native totem that was so common in the villages along the Alaskan coast. (Courtesy of the USCG Academy Museum.)

This picture is believed to be of members of the Overland Expedition. The person standing is probably Jarvis. Note the reindeer-hide outfits that kept them alive in temperatures as low as -70 degrees Fahrenheit. (Courtesy of USCG District No. 17 public information officer.)

Overland Expedition sleds are seen here taking supplies to stranded ships. (Courtesy of USCG District No. 17 public information officer.)

The Jarvis party arrived at Point Barrow on March 26, 1898, with 382 reindeer. The *Bear* broke through on July 28, not knowing what to expect. To their delight, they found that not a single whaler had been lost after Jarvis's arrival. An interesting footnote is that the participants had missed the entire Spanish-American War and knew nothing of it. (Courtesy of USCG District No. 17 public information officer.)

Sled dogs were important assets to the early ice operations. (Courtesy of University of Alaska, Fairbanks, Emile Krulish Collection.)

Jumping ahead 100 years, the Arctic ice was still claiming its victims. This time it was the fishing vessel *Alaskan Monarch* trapped in ice. An HH-3F helicopter from Kodiak successfully evacuated the crew. The vessel captain and engineer had elected to stay aboard and attempt to salvage the situation. They were swept overboard by an icy wave but saved from death by a helicopter crew that skillfully scooped them out of the icy waters. An interesting side note is that both the pilot and copilot were females. (Courtesy of USCG District No. 17 public information officer.)

Logistic support in the Arctic will increase as more players arrive. The author is on the *Northwind* flight deck with a tug and barge in the background. (Author's collection.)

Four

DOING ICEBREAKING THEN WITH CGC NORTHWIND

For a period of time, the Coast Guard had an assortment of icebreakers. Beginning in World War II, it became a priority to establish a fleet of icebreakers. During this period, the Wind class of icebreakers was constructed. These were the *Eastwind*, *Westwind*, *Southwind*, and *Northwind*. They were heavily armed and carried an amphibian aircraft. Of the four, the *Eastwind* and *Southwind* were the only ones to see active service during the war, both being involved with the capture of a German trawler in Greenland.

The *Southwind* had an interesting diversion during the war when she was loaned to the Russians from March 1945 until 1950, when she was returned to the United States. Originally serving as the US Navy icebreaker *Atka*, she was renamed USCGC *Southwind* (WAGB-280) when transferred to the Coast Guard in 1967. She was ultimately decommissioned in 1976 and sold.

Other US Navy icebreakers that were transferred to the Coast Guard were the USCGC *Burton Island* (WAGB-283), the USCGC *Edisto* (WAGB-284), and the USCGC *Glacier* (WAGB-4).

These icebreaking veterans were joined and/or replaced in 1976 by the USCGC *Polar Star* (WAGB-10) and *Polar Sea* (WAGB-11). These 400-foot heavyweights were considerably larger than the 269-foot Wind class. The latest addition to the icebreaking fleet is the USCGC *Healy* (WAGB-20), named for the famed Arctic veteran Mike Healy. For a period, the *Healy* was the only Arctic icebreaker active in the inventory. The icebreaker funding had been taken over by the National Science Foundation, and operating icebreakers took a cut due to lack of national priority. With the increasing activity in the Arctic, one of the Polar class was brought out of mothballs and is once again operational. The lead-time to build a new icebreaker is estimated to be 10 years.

What these important resources did in the Arctic will be demonstrated in this chapter by *Northwind* on its Arctic West deployment in 1967.

The enlisted aviation detachment from Coast Guard Air Station Astoria on the *Northwind* for the Arctic West–67 deployment kept the birds flying. From left to right are Aviation Electrician (AE)-2 John Furqueron, Aviation Machinist (AD)-2 Fred Todenhager, AE-3 Bob Hayden, Aviation Technician (AT)-2 Harold Watkins, and AD-1 George Baron, the lead petty officer. (Courtesy of AECS John Furqueron.)

Here, one of the two HH-13N helicopters comes aboard the *Northwind*. The second helicopter was named *Red Baron*. (Author's collection.)

Flight operations are conducted in the Inside Passage en route to Juneau and the first port call. Juneau is the headquarters of the Coast Guard in Alaska, and the *Northwind*'s operational control was maintained by the 17th District office in Juneau. (Author's collection.)

The federal office building in Juneau is where the majority of federal agencies in Alaska have their headquarters. The Coast Guard occupies two of the nine floors, and the operation center, which controls all operations in the district, is in this building. (Author's collection.)

Overlooking the Juneau Harbor is the governor's mansion on the hill. This is where the governor lives when in Juneau. (Author's collection.)

Northwind's executive officer, Cmdr. Stu Beckwith (left), and the author visit the Mendenhall Glacier. The glacier is approximately 15 miles outside Juneau in the Mendenhall Valley, where the majority of the families in the Juneau area live. The downtown area has limited buildable land due to the mountainous terrain. The few houses that are downtown are usually old and expensive. (Author's collection.)

Juneau was a popular destination even before statehood. The AJ or Alaska Juneau mine is on the hillside above the ships. (Courtesy of Alaska State Library, Robert DeArmond Collection.)

The *Northwind* steams into Dutch Harbor. This is the nearest support base at present for the Arctic ships. (Courtesy of Rear Adm. Doug Teeson.)

Pictured is the R/C *Tahoma*. She served on the Bering Sea Patrol from 1909 to 1914. On September 20, 1914, she struck an uncharted reef in the Aleutians and sank. Her crew was rescued by nearby vessels. (Courtesy of the USCG Academy Museum.)

Crew and officers of the *Tahoma* pose for a picture in Unalaska. (Courtesy of the USCG Academy Museum.)

The *Bear* is at home in the ice. It is amazing that this wooden ship had an operational life under the harshest of conditions for almost 70 years. This picture is from the scrapbook of crewman R.N. Hawley. (Courtesy of the USCG Academy Museum.)

Four Revenue Cutter officers enjoy a lighter moment with a seal pup. (Courtesy of the USCG Academy Museum.)

The cutter *Algonquin* is seen here with much of her crew visible off the coast of Seward, Alaska. (Courtesy of the USCG Academy Museum, Waesche Collection.)

The USRC *Perry* officers pose in their full dress aboard their ship in 1909. (Courtesy of the USCG Academy Museum.)

The three-story building is the original headquarters for the Coast Guard in Alaska. Following the end of World War II, the citizens of Juneau raised the funds for its construction hoping to lure the headquarters away from Ketchikan, where it was originally. It worked, and Ketchikan is still mad at Juneau for doing it. The old log building was at the time the home of the Juneau Visitors Center. The log cabin has since been demolished, and a small park is in its place. (Author's collection.)

Lt. Ron Addison, an aviator, returns from a flight in *Snoopy*. Frequent flight operations to get the ship's crew use to launching and recovering the helicopter were held. (Author's collection.)

Early in the deployment, different types of ice were encountered. One of the unusual ice types experienced was called "dirty ice." Whether this resulted from the ice having been aground at some time in its life or rather it was due to pollution falling on it over time is unknown. The bottom of the ice had algae build up on it, and as it was jumbled up over time, the bottoms were exposed. (Author's collection.)

Here, a King Islander is aboard the *Northwind* with his Umniat skin boat, which was used for hunting seals. (Courtesy of Rear Adm. Doug Teeson.)

Lt. Cmdr. Dick Burns, the senior aviator of the aviation detachment, had to go on emergency leave when his wife was in a serious automobile accident. Here, he is returning from emergency leave in style. The Navy H-2 was the aviation detachment on the *Glacier* and did the courtesy of delivering Dick by hoist. (Author's collection.)

Pictured are Lt. Cmdr. Dick Burns (left) and the author enjoying some fresh air on the *Northwind*. (Author's collection.)

Being gone from home for four months could get old. Crew members always looked for some diversions, such as this Saturday night poker game in the wardroom. (Author's collection.)

Another nice diversion was when Capt. Jim Phair, the *Northwind* commanding officer, presented promotion certificates in his quarters. From left to right are the author, Aviation Electrician Second Class (later Chief) John Furqueron, Captain Phair, and Lt. Ron Addison. (Author's collection.)

The enlisted crew of the aviation detachment had no problem coming up with forms of entertainment, including bringing lawn chairs to the flight deck. (Courtesy of AECS John Furqueron.)

However, the Arctic West deployment in 1967 had plenty of work to do. For part of its deployment, it was to coordinate operations with the Canadian icebreaker *Camsell*. Here, the operations officer of the *Northwind*, Lt. Paul Scherer, goes aboard the *Camsell* to confer with his counterpart concerning the upcoming DEW Line resupply know as the McKenzie River Sealift. (Author's collection.)

A half dozen times during the deployment, the *Northwind* became stuck and had to use dynamite to assist in breaking loose. The procedure was to go full astern, heeling system on, and on a signal, blast away. It seldom had any effect, but it put on a great show. (Author's collection.)

The setting of the shaped charges was not rocket science. A hole had to be dug in the ice with a pick and then as many as 10 charges were placed around the ship. (Courtesy of Rear Adm. Doug Teeson.)

The *Northwind* had a team of qualified divers who were used occasionally to check out the underside of the vessel, primarily the huge propellers, for damage. (Author's collection.)

The helicopter here was assisting the divers in their investigation. (Courtesy of Rear Adm. Doug Teeson.)

It never got old getting off the ship to walk on the ice, and when land and time were available, a friendly game of ball would sometimes be played. (Courtesy of AECS John Furqueron.)

The flight crews had an advantage in that they were often required to fly ashore to pick up mail or supplies and were able to check out different places. Alcoholism is a problem with the Native

Having good meals served to the crew was another way to keep morale up. Unfortunately, early in the deployment, fresh vegetables ran out and canned milk had to be used. Occasionally, there would be a special event, like celebrating the captain's birthday. The captain normally ate alone in his cabin and had his own steward, but in this case, he was invited to be a guest of the wardroom. (Author's collection.)

people. At times there were occurrences of Eskimos draining the antifreeze from the contract company vehicles and drinking it. Note the Eskimo crossing sign. (Author's collection.)

This is a picture of Point Barrow in 1967. The Naval Research Laboratory (NARL) there was an important logistical facility. One very important item before the days of satellites and cell phones was the ship's mail, which was flown into Barrow. (Author's collection.)

The NARL had a very nice collection of Eskimo ceremonial masks. (Author's collection.)

An important mission of the Arctic West deployment in 1967 was the oceanographic research done by the guest scientists and ship's oceanographic personnel. This required the ship to anchor in a set pattern for several weeks while water samples were taken at different levels utilizing a Nansen bottle, as shown here. While important, this was a crushing bore for the flight crews as there were no associated flight operations required other than to bring aboard the scientists and return them to an airstrip following the period. (Author's collection.)

The land in the background is Russia. This photograph, taken from the flight deck of the *Northwind*, shows how narrow the straits are in this location. The unique rock formation is Fairway Rock. (Courtesy of AECS John Furqueron.)

Another mission that was a lot more fun was the Fairway Rock strontium-90 generator recharging. An earlier mission had established underwater sensors to measure the water flow and properties in the adjacent straits to the rock. A generator on the top of the 500-foot monolith powered the system. It was the aviation detachment's job to take technicians to the top of the rock to recharge the generator. The 500,000 or so birds that called Fairway Rock home were not pleased with the intrusion. (Courtesy of AECS John Furqueron.)

A diversion that was not on the schedule was the distress call of the Canadian research ship *Richardson*, which was trapped in the ice. This required the *Northwind* to make best speed in the ice, similar to this earlier picture of this Wind class icebreaker smashing ice. (Courtesy of Dr. Robert Browning, Coast Guard Headquarters historian.)

Both helicopters, shown here in their stowed position, were launched once *Northwind* was near the distress to locate the hapless vessel. (Courtesy of AECS John Furqueron.)

The Canadian research ship *Richardson* was trapped in the clutches of the Arctic. (Courtesy of AECS John Furqueron.)

The Canadian icebreaker *Camsell* also responded to the distress but was unable to break through to the *Richardson*; *Camsell* stood by as the more powerful *Northwind* broke her out. (Author's collection.)

The *Northwind* then opened things up in order to escort both the *Camsell* and *Richardson* to open water and safety so that each could proceed independently. (Courtesy of AECS John Furqueron.)

The crews on the *Camsell* and *Richardson* were glad to have the *Northwind*'s assistance. (Courtesy of AECS John Furqueron.)

The meat-and-potatoes of the Arctic West deployment in 1967 was support for the DEW Line resupply. Here, a tug and barge are seen doing the actual resupply. The *Northwind*'s function was to be available for inadvertent ice encounters. (Courtesy of Ned Lofton.)

Another main goal of the deployment was to resupply of the manned floating ice island nicknamed T-3. On it were a large number of scientists and technical people doing research. The five-mile-long island floated around the Arctic and needed to be resupplied periodically. This was normally done by air, but in 1967, an icebreaker attempted to do it. The problem was that because of the different assistance cases and other duties, the *Northwind* got started one month later than planned, and the ice was forming. Part of the logistics required loading hundreds of 55-gallon barrels of fuel and lubricants that had to be offloaded every time the ship was sent on another rescue mission. This was done three times before the T-3 resupply mission started. (Author's collection.)

Spending a lot of time at Point Barrow had its advantages. These polar bears were being studied, as were several wolves and other Arctic animals. (Courtesy of AECS John Furqueron.)

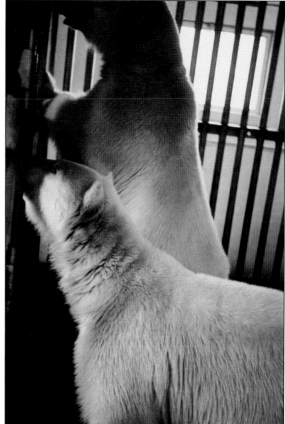

This monument marks the location of the plane crash that killed aviator Wally Post and writer and entertainer Will Rogers. It occurred when the plane was taking off from a nearby lagoon, a short distance from Point Barrow, in August 1935. (Courtesy of AECS John Furqueron.)

Pictured here is a very happy Eskimo girl from Point Barrow named Mukpie. According to the photographer's notes, she was the youngest passenger ever aboard this unnamed Canadian vessel. (Courtey of the USCG Academy Museum.)

Of course, the greatest attraction at Point Barrow was the ship's mail that was flown in there and picked up by helicopter. Those who flew the helicopters were very popular when they returned to the ship. (Author's collection.)

Heading for T-3, those on deployment made good time initially. Crew members would at regular intervals set off charges for the scientists on T-3 to ascertain the speed of sound traveling in the Arctic conditions. (Author's collection.)

The easy ice soon gave way to the tough, weathered kind, which slowed down travel. Personnel were placed on the ice to inspect the hull or to gather information. (Courtesy of Ned Lofton.)

It was a pretty lonely place on the ice. A Navy P-3 aircraft on ice patrol was a welcome diversion. Often, they would drop magazines and newspapers, which were eagerly read by all. (Author's collection.)

The ice finally got too much for the *Northwind*'s capabilities. The mission was canceled and the ship was directed to abandon the effort and head south to better conditions. (Author's collection.)

While backing down, the ship sheered a blade off the starboard propeller, leaving the *Northwind* with only one usable shaft. Attempts to use the damaged one caused extreme vibrations that could have caused even more damage. The picture was taken in dry dock after the vessel's return. (Courtesy of Rear Adm. Doug Teeson.)

With conditions worsening, the *Northwind*'s ability to break ice was restricted, which is not a good combination. The decision was made to declare an emergency. The only way to help an icebreaker in trouble is with another icebreaker. The icebreaker *Glacier* was directed to depart from Long Beach, California, where she was preparing for an Antarctic deployment, to assist *Northwind*. The Canadian icebreaker *John A. MacDonald*, nicknamed *Johnnie Mac*, was also requested. (Author's collection.)

The arrival of the two breakers two weeks later was a pretty sight. Prior to the icebreakers' arrival, it was decided that a team of about 17 engineering personnel, headed by Lt. (j.g.) Doug Teeson, the damage control assistant, would have had to stay with the ship over the winter. Planning meetings had already started. The remainder of the crew would be removed by aircraft on skis. (Author's collection.)

Following the *Northwind*'s return to her home port in Seattle, she was placed in a dry dock to accomplish repairs to her damaged propeller. (Courtesy of Rear Adm. Doug Teeson.)

Northwind's crew worked with the *Johnnie Mac* and her helicopter, sharing the flight time so that there was always a helicopter scouting ahead. The author of this book is pictured flying. At times, pilots would take members of the crew as observers; during the flight pictured, Lt (j.g.) Doug Teeson was a passenger. (Courtesy of Rear Adm. Doug Teeson.)

It is interesting to compare the launch of a Canadian helicopter with procedures used by the US Coast Guard. The Canadian pilot often flew with his German shepherd in the copilot seat. Their launch crew consisted of one guy to help push the helicopter out of the hangar. *Northwind*'s aviation detachment, on the other hand, had about 40 people, such as crash crews, manning a lifeboat, and communications talkers. (Courtesy of Rear Adm. Doug Teeson.)

Five

DELIVERY TO THE DEW LINE

The Distance Early Warning stations in Alaska and the Canadian Arctic were a tribute to man's ability to do difficult things in dangerous places when defense was involved. From 1955 to 1957, the stations were constructed as a defense against a Soviet bomber attack over the pole. The manned stations had one function, which was to scan the sky electronically to be able to detect inbound aircraft. These extremely remote sites were manned with approximately 40 civilian technicians with a military liaison officer. Their primary means of logistical support was by sealift to bring in bulk fuel and supplies. In the late summer, the ice would normally retreat from the shore adequately to allow tugs and barges and supply vessels access to the stations. As often happened, however, the wind would shift, blowing the ice back in and trapping the supply ships—enter the icebreaker to release them.

A lonely DEW Line station sits on a bluff over a sea of ice. (Courtesy of Ned Lofton.)

One of the resupply vessels, the *Pinnebog*, became stuck in ice and requested the *Northwind*'s assistance. (Author's collection.)

On approach to the top of Fairway Rock, Russia can be seen in the background. (Courtesy of AECS John Furqueron.)

Here is a beautiful shot of the *Northwind* sailing into Dutch Harbor. (Courtesy of AECS John Furqueron.)

The multiyear ice, as seen here, is always present. The wind moves it to and from the shoreline, making any operation risky, in this case entrapping the Canadian research ship *Richardson*. (Courtesy of Rear Adm. Doug Teeson.)

The best insurance was to have an icebreaker available when delivering supplies. (Author's collection.)

Visits to the DEW Line stations were good for the morale of the isolated crews. (Author's collection.)

The pontoons on the H-13, seen here in the center of the photograph, gave it a safe footprint on the ice. (Author's collection.)

The *Northwind* provided a great platform for Arctic research, resupply, and rescues in the ice, but the personnel at the isolated DEW Line stations were dependent on the supplies and heating fuel that the sealift provided and the *Northwind* facilitated. (Courtesy of Rear Adm. Doug Teeson.)

The Wind-class icebreakers are all gone, as are the *Edisto, Staten Island, Burton Island*, and *Glacier*. Likewise, the DEW Line is a thing of the past. The beauty and challenges of the Arctic remain. (Courtesy of AECS John Furqueron.)

Six

Doing Icebreaking Now with CGC *Healy* and CGC *Polar Sea*

From the glory days of the Arctic West deployment in 1967, when the Coast Guard had as many as eight icebreakers (*Storis, Eastwind, Southwind, Westwind, Northwind, Edisto, Burton Island, Staten Island*), the fleet went to only one medium icebreaker, the *Healy*, in operation and two Polar-class icebreakers in mothballs. There are several reasons why the fleet grew smaller, but the primary one is lack of a national resolve to have a realistic national icebreaking capability. The *Polar Star* was brought back to life in 2012 with a seven-year life extension. The United States is still way behind the icebreaker power curve. Russia has 24. The United States needs to do better if it is going to be prepared for all the increased activity that is forecasted for the Arctic.

In the picture, the author's late wife, Sylvia, right, and Ens. Rebekah Follmer, the USCGC *Healy* public information officer, pose before the *Healy* on a visit to the ship in the yard. At 420 feet in length overall, the *Healy* is over 150 feet longer than the *Northwind*, and her displacement of 16,000 tons is nearly three times that of the *Northwind*. She was the largest ship ever built for the Coast Guard. She was designed to break 4.5 feet of ice at a steady three knots and nearly 8 feet by backing and ramming. (Author's collection.)

The *Healy* is moored in Dutch Harbor. Dutch Harbor played an important role in the Bering Sea patrol days as a coaling station. The area also saw action when a Japanese aircraft carrier attacked Dutch Harbor on June 3, 1942. As operations increase in the Arctic, Dutch Harbor will play an important part as one of the few refueling ports in the Aleutians. (Courtesy of Ens. Rebecca Follmer, CGC *Healy* public information officer.)

The *Polar Star* (WAGB-10) and the *Polar Sea* (WAGB-11) joined the Coast Guard fleet in 1976. At 399 feet, they were designed to break 6.5 feet of ice at three knots. They could also do 18 knots in open water. Both parameters were considerably greater than the Wind-class icebreakers they replaced; however, there were only two icebreakers to replace eight. This beautiful model in Coast Guard Museum Northwest clearly shows the unique bow. (Author's collection.)

The Polar-class sisters are tied up at Pier No. 36 in Seattle, yearning for the Arctic. (Author's collection.)

On Coast Guard Day on August 4, 1990, the Bering Sea Patrol Memorial was dedicated at Dutch Harbor. Sen. Frank Murkowski, later Alaska governor and earlier a petty officer in the Coast Guard, played a key role in the memorial's dedication. (Author's collection.)

The author places a wreath on the grave of a Revenue Cutter sailor from the Bering Sea days on Coast Guard Day in 1990. The Coast Guard personnel in period uniforms are from the fabled cutter *Storis*, a veteran of the successful crossing of the Northwest Passage and the principle mover in the Bering Sea Monument project. At the time of this picture, the *Storis* was the oldest commissioned cutter in the Coast Guard. (Courtesy of USCG District No. 17 public information officer.)

Late in 2011, Nome was facing a crisis. Due to bad storms, the fuel barge had not gotten in by the end of the season, and the fuel for the community would be exhausted in the middle of the winter. Congress requested Adm. Robert Papp Jr., the 24th commandant of the Coast Guard, to divert the CGC *Healy* (WAGB-20) to assist with getting a fuel barge or tanker into Nome. With the ice rapidly forming, the plan was to do it by a Russian ice-reinforced tanker. (Courtesy of Ens. Rebecca Follmer, CGC *Healy* public information officer.)

The *Healy* proceeded to Dutch Harbor, where she picked up an interpreter and a Coast Guard aviation detachment. The Russian skipper of the *Renda* and Capt. Beverly Havlik of the *Healy* met to plan the relief mission. (Courtesy of Ens. Rebecca Follmer, CGC *Healy* public information officer.)

The *Healy* leads the *Renda* to Nome with the precious cargo of heating oil. (Courtesy of Ens. Rebecca Follmer, CGC *Healy* public information officer.)

The *Renda* pumps her load of heating oil across the ice to the Nome fuel tanks using miles of hose. (Courtesy of Ens. Rebecca Follmer, CGC *Healy* public information officer.)

On May 2, 2013, the changing of the guard occurred aboard the *Healy*. Capt. John Reeves relieved Capt. Beverly Havlik, who had been commanding officer since April 2011. Reeves was well qualified for the command, having previously served as the *Healy* executive officer and engineering officer. One adverse result in the reduction in the number of operational icebreakers is that the pool of experienced ice sailors, like Havlik and Reeves, is greatly diminished. (Courtesy of Ens. Rebecca Follmer, CGC *Healy* public information officer.)

Cmdr. Stu Beckwith overlooks the sea of ice. This image captures one of the many faces of ice with which the mission had to contend. The Eskimos have almost 100 words to describe different types of ice. (Author's collection.)

Petty Officer Hayden stands in front of the HH-13s that were replaced on the *Healy* by HH-65A Dolphins. Dedicated helicopter crews are now a thing of the past with the loss of expertise that had been gained over the years of operations. (Author's collection.)

Seven

DUTIES OF THE COAST
GUARD IN THE ARCTIC

The Coast Guard has 11 mission areas by law. These are as follows: 1) Ports, waterways, and coastal security, 2) Drug interdiction, 3) Aids to navigation, 4) Search and rescue, 5) Living marine resource, 6) Marine safety, 7) Defense readiness, 8) Migrant interdiction, 9) Marine environment protection, 10) Ice operations, and 11) Other law enforcement.

Some of these missions are more challenging in the Arctic than others. For example, Merchant vessel safety is going to be a considerable problem when cruise ships with thousands of passengers venture into the Far North, where rescue capabilities are limited or nonexistent.

Likewise, aids to navigation are critical in an area where the sea bottoms are unknown or only partially charted. However, establishing traditional aids, such as buoys, would have to be seasonal lest the winter ice destroy them.

The traditional search-and-rescue mission would likewise be difficult with no deepwater port north of the Aleutians and the only permanent air station being at Kodiak nearly 1,000 miles from Barrow. This is a mission that calls for formal international protocols to assist any mariner in distress in these lonely oceans.

The marine environmental protection mission will become of great importance as the search for oil is expanded into the offshore areas. Handling a spill presents daunting challenges when available resources are far away.

The traditional law enforcement mission will see increased emphasis as more open water leads to more fisheries with the associated need to board and inspect vessels from many nations.

The study of the impact on this sensitive area by the increased commerce coupled with the changes brought by global warming will reinforce the need for marine science research to determine causes and effects.

The *Bear*, shown here under sail, was often involved in the law enforcement mission. She protected marine mammals from being exploited. The most famous of the captains of the *Bear* was Mike Healy, who had taken command in 1886 and was given the orders to "seize any vessel found sealing in the Bering Sea." (Courtesy of the USCG Academy Museum.)

The *Bear*, at 200 feet in length with a beam of 32 feet, was not particularly large, but she was ruggedly built for the rigors of the Arctic. (Courtesy of AECS John Furqueron.)

Often the law enforcement duties of the Coast Guard require international diplomatic coordination, such as in this case where Revenue Cutter sailors are holding Japanese fishermen for fishing violations. (Courtesy of the USCG Academy Museum, Waesche Collection.)

The enforcement of order against sealing in the Pribiloffs was one of the earliest and most controversial of the mission mix. Here is a valuable lot of seal skins. (Courtesy of the USCG Academy Museum, Rush/Shepard Collection.)

The service had many dealings with the Eskimos. Supplies were delivered; medical help was provided; missionaries were supported. Here, the *Bear* is in the background. (Courtesy of the USCG Academy Museum, Rush/Shepard Collection.)

The chief's house at Point Hope on the Arctic Ocean is shown here. Mainly underground, it has logs, sod, and whalebones as needed. (Courtesy of the USCG Academy Museum, Claude Merrow Collection.)

Another legal authority for the Revenue Cutter captains, but one that was more enjoyable, was marrying Alaskan Natives. (Courtesy of USCG District No. 17 public information officer.)

The use of the revenue cutters to assist and protect the Native Alaskans was an important function, but one that does not readily fit into the traditional mission descriptions. These were often called "cooperation with other agencies" missions, also known as COOP missions. The establishment of reindeer for the Native schools fits into the COOP mission. The original caption by an unknown archivist probably should have given the credit for the picture to the Loman brothers, who were reindeer entrepreneurs during the Nome gold rush. (Courtesy of Alaska State Library, David Brower Collection.)

One of the more unusual duties was the assignment of the revenue cutter *Nunivak* to patrol the thousand-mile-long Yukon River during the gold rush into the Canadian Yukon. Her mission was to keep law and order and to assist those in distress. (Courtesy of USCG District No. 17 public information officer.)

The ship would be placed in a berm and frozen over in the winter. The crew maintained good order and discipline by performing close order drills on the frozen Yukon. (Courtesy of USCG District No. 17 public information officer.)

As the Arctic sees more activity, the need for more international cooperation will be increased. Here, the USCGC *Northwind* assists the Canadian *Camsell*. Later during the Arctic West cruise, the Canadian icebreaker *John A. McDonald* returned the favor by breaking out the *Northwind* following damage to a ship's screw. (Courtesy of Ned Lofton.)

This picture of the *Bear* is a reminder being trapped by ice is always a risk when ice is present. Accordingly, resources for assistance will also be needed, especially as maritime activity increases. (Courtesy of Alaska State Library, Robert Pittenger Collection.)

Any mission in the ice requires an icebreaker. Here, a sailor watches the CGC *Glacier* approach through the ice. Both of these icebreakers are no more and were not replaced. (Author's collection.)

These "bergy bits," as they are known, are a long way from the Arctic. This is Icy Bay, located west of Yakutat in southeast Alaska. The ice nevertheless makes coming ashore in a small boat hazardous. Accordingly, a helicopter was required to bring in aids-to-navigation personnel to service a navigational aid that was built here. Likewise, the formation of ice can affect all of Alaska's ports. This is of importance when one remembers that 90 percent of what the United States consumes travels by sea. (Author's collection.)

These three sailing ships are anchored in Dutch Harbor on Unalaska in the Aleutians. Amazingly, this is the nearest US port for supplies and fuel to the Arctic. From here to Point Barrow would be three days sailing for most Coast Guard cutters. (Courtesy of Alaska State Library, Samuel J. Call Collection.)

Pictured here is the Dutch Harbor US Navy Aero Unit Headquarters held over from World War II. (Courtesy of AECS John Furqueron.)

The helicopter and rescue swimmer team, as shown here, has saved many lives. To have these capabilities available in the Arctic is going to take some extensive development of support infrastructure, such as hangars, which are presently not available. (Author's collection.)

The HH-13N *Red Baron* from the *Northwind* in 1967 is seen in front of the Naval Arctic Research Laboratory Hangar. These hangars are no longer functional. (Courtesy of AECS John Furqueron.)

This unfortunate picture shows Revenue Cutter personnel at the Cape Hope Graveyard demonstrating a lack of respect for those buried there. Those in authority must not tolerate such behavior. (Courtesy of the USCG Academy Museum UID AEBD 6.)

A major oil spill in the Arctic is a nightmare to contemplate. The cleanup following the *Exxon Valdez* grounding, shown here, involved thousands of personnel, tons of equipment, and hundreds of vessels over a three-year period. Getting resources in these numbers in the Arctic and then trying to support them there is not possible. (Courtesy of USCG District No. 17 public information officer.)

The reindeer sled was an innovation of its day in Nome for handling mail delivery and basic logistics. The development of the Arctic without serious disruption to the traditional ways of life of the indigenous people will be a challenge. (Courtesy of Alaska State Library, George Family Collection.)

The impact of increased activity in the Arctic on the indigenous animals will also need to be factored in. (Courtesy of Alaska State Library, US Revenue Cutter Service Collection.)

The author shows daughter Nicole a Kodiak king crab on Marginal Pier at Kodiak Support Center. There is potential for fisheries developing in the Arctic. The king crab population around Kodiak Island is a case study of what happens if a fishery is not managed adequately. Kings were common and easily caught from piers in the 1960s and 1970s, but overfishing commercially greatly depleted this resource. As more open water in the Arctic develops for longer periods of time, a fishery is likely to grow that must be enforced by the Coast Guard. (Author's collection.)

As activity increases in the Arctic, so should the Coast Guard increase its presence with ships and aviation detachments. As was the case with Arctic West, these detachments must be capable of sustained operations a long way from home. (Courtesy of University of Alaska, Fairbanks, R.S. Leusen Collection.)

Increasingly, the need for international cooperation and sharing of responsibilities will be required. This will happen only if the national agenda sees it as a priority now and not wait for a disaster to be the reason for the attention. (Courtesy of AECS John Furqueron.)

The challenges are there as well as the opportunities. The overall goal must be to ensure that whatever happens today does not destroy the Arctic's future. (Courtesy of AECS John Furqueron.)

Eight

DESTINY OF THE ARCTIC

What does the future portend in the Arctic? Can it be predicted based on the past? What we have learned is certainly a place to start. But things are changing. The ice is retreating farther and sooner and coming back later. Where there were few who ventured here in the past, there are now many. The modern Coast Guard cutter *Bertholf* on patrol in the Arctic in the summer of 2012 reported having 95 contacts on her radar in one 24-hour period. There are new players in the snow pile.

In August 2012, the Chinese icebreaker *Snow Dragon* made a successful transit of the Northwest Passage. The Chinese government has also applied for permanent observer status on the Arctic Council. The diamonds of the Arctic are exerting their allure.

The Arctic can be dangerous and unpredictable. There is much unknown about it. It is universally known that there are resources of great value if they can be harvested safely. There are many players, but there is only one playing field. Are the rules equally followed? Who will enforce them without violating sovereign rights on the part of the individual players? What can be predicted about this wonderful place?

There will still be ice to contend with for the majority of the year. A vessel in the ice must be strong enough if it is trapped. (Courtesy of AECS John Furqueron.)

The support for vessels operating in the Arctic is over 1,000 miles away at present. The only place to refuel today is in the Aleutians, where the *Northwind* is seen steaming. A deepwater harbor must be developed closer to where the operations will be. (Courtesy of AECS John Furqueron.)

There will need to be extensive studies and diplomatic initiatives sponsored, like the Leadership for the Arctic Seminar, which was cosponsored by the US Coast Guard Academy, shown here, and the University of California, Berkeley, in April 2012. (Author's collection.)

An important consideration in all discussions is the impact on the indigenous peoples of the Arctic. (Courtesy of the Coast Guard Northwest Museum.)

When ice is present or there is a possibility for ice, an icebreaker needs to be available for assistance when required. The United States, with only two icebreakers, has limited response capability. Icebreakers need yard time following deployments, and there is no yard in Alaska capable of accommodating a vessel the size of an icebreaker. (Courtesy of AECS John Furqueron.)

Cooperation between nations will be required to handle emergencies or to prevent them. Here, the Canadian icebreaker *John A. McDonald* assists the damaged *Northwind*. The *McDonald* received a commendation from the commandant of the US Coast Guard for her heroic efforts on the *Northwind*'s behalf. (Courtesy of AECS John Furqueron.)

The lifestyle of the Eskimos has adapted to the realities of today while keeping what was good from the past. Using a pickup truck to transport a native skin kayak is a good example. (Courtesy of AECS John Furqueron.)

Here, a ship assists an Eskimo with butchering and dressing a sea lion that he had shot. The meat was brought aboard by cargo net. (Courtesy of Rear Adm. Doug Teeson.)

A party looks for bird eggs in the Pribiloff Islands. (Courtesy of the USCG Academy Museum.)

From an operational point of view, the helicopters were the eyes of the ship in the ice. Helicopters could determine what route was best to avoid heading down a lead into an impassable pressure ridge. The need for the icebreaker helicopter team will be even more important as the numbers and diversity of activities increase. With a 10-year lead time to produce a replacement for the *Northwind*, the Coast Guard is already behind before it has even started. (Courtesy of AECS John Furqueron.)

The long history of dedicated humanitarian service in the Arctic needs to be continued. This old photograph shows the US Lifesaving Service (USLS) lifeboat station at Nome. The USLS was the forerunner of the Coast Guard, which was formed from the combining of the Lifesaving Service and the Revenue Cutter Service in 1915. (Courtesy of the Coast Guard Museum Northwest.)

Just as the icebreakers have moved on, so have the men who fixed them and operated them. Shown here is then–Lt. (j.g.) Doug Teeson, who was a damage control officer for the Arctic West deployment in 1967. (Author's collection.)

Here is a portrait of Rear Adm. Doug Teeson; at the time of the portrait, he was the superintendent of the Coast Guard Academy. He has since retired. (Author's collection.)

The Arctic's future is not so different from the Arctic's past. It will still play host to men overcoming challenges with the means at hand. As Admiral Nimitz once said, "Amateurs talk tactics, professionals talk logistics." (Courtesy of Alaska State Library p134a-Bear-01 Robert DeArmond Photograph Collection.)

There may be a pot of gold at the end of the Arctic rainbow, but getting the pot without negatively impacting this beautiful, dangerous, and critically important place will not be easy. (Courtesy of Rear Adm. Doug Teeson.)

BIBLIOGRAPHY

Alaska Economic Trends. Juneau: Alaska Department of Labor and Workforce Development, 2011.

Beard, Tom, ed. *The Coast Guard*. Seattle; Hugh Lauther Levin Associates, Inc., 2004.

Borneman, Walter R. *Alaska: Saga of a Bold Land*. New York: HarperCollins Publishers, Inc., 2003.

Cohen, Stan. *The Great Alaska Pipeline*. Missoula: Pictorial Histories Publishing Co., 1988.

——. *8.6 The Great Alaska Earthquake*. Missoula: Pictorial Histories Publishing Co., 1995.

——. *The Streets Were Paved with Gold*. Missoula: Pictorial Histories Publishing Co., 1977.

——. *The Forgotten War*. Missoula: Pictorial Histories Publishing Co., 1981.

Costello, John. *Days of Infamy*. New York: Pocket Books, 1994.

Davidson, Art. *In the Wake of the Exxon Valdez*. San Francisco: Sierra Club Books, 1990.

Ferrell, Nancy Warren. *Alaska's Heroes: A Call to Courage*. Portland, OR: Alaska Northwest Books, 2002.

Garfield, Brian. *The Thousand-Mile War*. New York: Bantam Books, 1988.

Gates, Nancy, ed. *The Alaska Almanac: Facts about Alaska*. 32nd ed. Portland, OR: Alaska Northwest Books, 2008.

Helvarg, David. *Rescue Warrior*. New York: Thomas Dunne Books, St. Martin's Press, 2009.

Jeffers, H. Paul. *Burning Cold*. St. Paul: Zenith Press, 2006.

Kaplan, H.R., and Lt. Cmdr. James F. Hunt, USCG. *This Is the Coast Guard*. Cambridge, MD: Cornell Maritime Press, Inc., 1972.

Kroll, C. Douglas. *Commodore Ellsworth P. Bertholf*. Annapolis: Naval Institute Press, 2002.

LaGuardia-Kotite, Martha J. *So Others May Live*. Guilford, CT: The Lyons Press, 2006.

Lebedoff, David. *Cleaning Up*. New York: The Free Press, 1997.

Noble, Dennis L. *Alaska and Hawaii: A Brief History of Coast Guard Operations*. Washington DC: Coast Guard Historian's Office, 1991.

Noble, Dennis L., and Truman R. Strobridge. *Captain "Hell Roaring" Mike Healy*. Gainesville: University Press of Florida, 2009.

Prange, George W. *At Dawn We Slept*. New York: McGraw-Hill Book Company, 1981.

Reeves, Lt. Gen. R.J., USAF. *Operation Helping Hand*. Anchorage: Headquarters Alaska Command, 1964.

Rigge, Simon. *War in the Outposts*. Alexandria, VA: Time-Life Books, 1980.

Schoel, Cmdr. Richard L., USCG. *M/V Prinsendam SAR Case Study*. Juneau: CCGD17 (osr).

Skinner, Samuel K., and William K. Reilly. *The Exxon Valdez Oil Spill*. Washington, DC: National Response Team, May 1989.

Strobridge, Truman R., and Dennis L. Noble. *Alaska and the US Revenue Cutter Service 1867–1915*. Annapolis: Naval Institute Press, 1999.

Taliaerro, John. *In a Far Country*. New York: Public Affairs Books, 2006.

DISCOVER THOUSANDS OF LOCAL HISTORY BOOKS FEATURING MILLIONS OF VINTAGE IMAGES

Arcadia Publishing, the leading local history publisher in the United States, is committed to making history accessible and meaningful through publishing books that celebrate and preserve the heritage of America's people and places.

Find more books like this at
www.arcadiapublishing.com

Search for your hometown history, your old stomping grounds, and even your favorite sports team.

Consistent with our mission to preserve history on a local level, this book was printed in South Carolina on American-made paper and manufactured entirely in the United States. Products carrying the accredited Forest Stewardship Council (FSC) label are printed on 100 percent FSC-certified paper.

MADE IN THE USA